Animals Close Up

FISH CLOSE UP

I0811286

By Seth Lynch

Gareth Stevens
PUBLISHING

Please visit our website, www.garethstevens.com. For a free color catalog of all our high-quality books, call toll free 1-800-542-2595 or fax 1-877-542-2596.

Library of Congress Cataloging-in-Publication Data
Names: Lynch, Seth, author.
Title: Fish close up / Seth Lynch.
Description: New York : Gareth Stevens Publishing, [2023] | Series: Animals close up | Includes index.
Identifiers: LCCN 2021040549 (print) | LCCN 2021040550 (ebook) | ISBN 9781538281284 (set) | ISBN 9781538281291 (library binding) | ISBN 9781538281277 (paperback) | ISBN 9781538281307 (ebook)
Subjects: LCSH: Fishes–Juvenile literature.
Classification: LCC QL617.2 .L96 2023 (print) | LCC QL617.2 (ebook) | DDC 597–dc23
LC record available at https://lccn.loc.gov/2021040549
LC ebook record available at https://lccn.loc.gov/2021040550

First Edition

Published in 2023 by
Gareth Stevens Publishing
29 East 21st Street
New York, NY 10010

Editor: Kristen Nelson
Designer: Rachel Rising

Photo credits: Cover, p. 1 New Africa/Shutterstock.com; p. 5 Ingrid Prats/Shutterstock.com; p. 7 Martin Voeller/Shutterstock.com; p. 9 Elocphotos/Shutterstock.com; p.11 dive-hive/Shutterstock.com; p. 13 Lotus_studio/Shutterstock.com; p. 15 Glass and Nature/Shuttestock.com; pp. 17, 24 DmZ/Shutterstock.com; p. 19 Noheaphotos/Shutterstock.com; pp. 21, 24 Napat/Shutterstock.com; p. 23, 24 ThomasLENNE/Shutterstock.com.

Printed in the United States of America

CPSIA compliance information: Batch #CSGS23: For further information contact Gareth Stevens, New York, New York at 1-800-542-2595.

Contents

Fish are amazing animals! There are thousands of kinds.

Sharks are fish!

Fish can be small or big.

The whale shark is
the biggest.

Fish live in the water.

Sunfish live in lakes.

Fish can breathe
in water.
They use gills.

They have two eyes.
Many cannot see far.

Most fish have scales.
They cover the body.

Fish have fins.
Fins help them move.

Words to Know

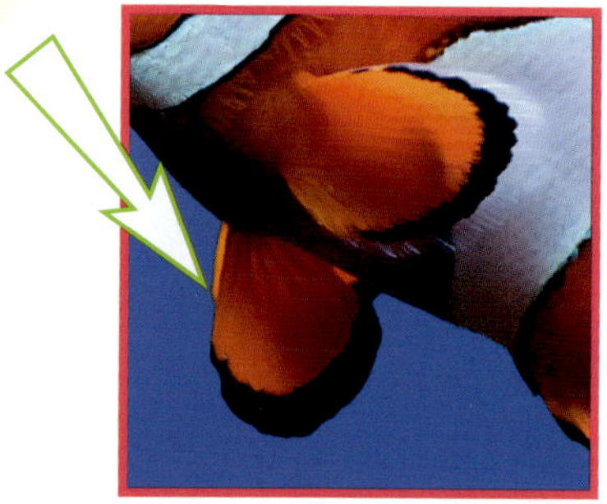

fin

gills

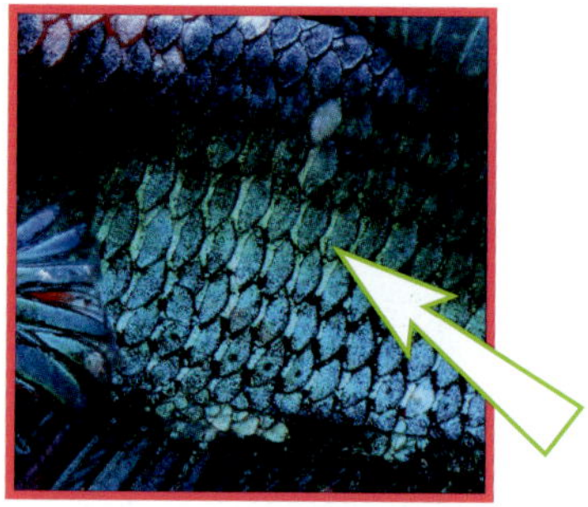

scales

Index